"The harvest truly is plenteous, but the labourers are few;
Pray ye therefore the Lord of the harvest, that He will send forth labourers into His harvest."
— Matthew 9:37–38

DR. LETITIA MCPHERSON

IT'S REVIVAL TIME

TO

FROM

"The fire of revival does not fall where it is admired, but where it is prepared for."

Dr. Letitia McPherson

It's Revival Time

Why Some Churchs Will Miss It

Dr. Letitia McPherson

No part of this publication may be reproduced, distributed, or transmitted in any form or by any means, including photocopying, recording, or other electronic or mechanical methods, without the prior written permission of the publisher, except in the case of brief quotations embodied in critical reviews and certain other non - commercial uses permitted by copyright law.
Scripture quotations are taken from the KJV and the NIV Translation * of the Bible, unless otherwise noted, and are used by permission. All rights reserved.
For permission requests, write to the publisher at: Dr. Letitia McPherson
Email: bishopmcpherson@gmail.com
Based in North York, Ontario Canada
ISBN: 978-1-990266-76-8
Printed in the USA by Amazon
Copyright © 2026 by Dr. Letitia McPherson
All rights reserved.

TABLE OF CONTENTS

Dedication
Author's Note
Introduction – Before My Feet Touched the Floor

SECTION I — WHY REVIVAL IS MISSED

Chapter 1
When Comfort Becomes an Idol
HOW EASE SILENCES THE CRY FOR MORE

Chapter 2
When Image Replaces Glory
CHOOSING APPEARANCE OVER THE WEIGHT OF HIS PRESENCE

Chapter 3
The Pride That Silences Repentance
WHEN LEADERS CANNOT BOW, REVIVAL CANNOT FLOW

Chapter 4
Control vs the Move of the Spirit
WHEN ORDER IS USED TO RESTRAIN THE SPIRIT

Chapter 5
Entertainment and the Golden Calf Church
WHEN PERFORMANCE REPLACES THE PRESENCE OF GOD

Chapter 6
A Church Without a Burden for Souls
WHEN THE HARVEST IS FORGOTTEN, THE FIRE FADES

Chapter 7
Tradition
THE RESPECTABLE RESISTANCE

Chapter 8
Why Revival Moves Elsewhere
WHEN READINESS DETERMINES RESTING PLACES

SECTION II — UNDERSTANDING REVIVAL

Chapter 9
The Nature of Revival Fire
WHAT REVIVAL IS AND WHAT IT IS NOT

Chapter 10
The Cost of Revival
WHAT FIRE REQUIRES BEFORE IT FALLS

Chapter 11
Preparing the Altar Again
RETURNING TO THE PLACE WHERE FIRE FALLS

SECTION III — THE INVITATION

Chapter 12
It Is Not Too Late
THE DOOR OF MERCY IS STILL OPEN

Epilogue – A Prayer for the Altar
About the Author

DEDICATION

To every heart that still hungers.

To the quiet intercessors who pray when no one sees.

To the leaders who carry holy burden for the flock.

To the believers who long not for noise, but for nearness.

To those who refuse comfort when God is calling deeper.

To every soul who still whispers, "Lord, come again."

This book is dedicated to the revival seekers — those who desire not the appearance of fire, but the presence of God.

May your hunger never fade.
May your altar never grow cold.
May your cry help usher in the hour we have been waiting for.

AUTHOR'S NOTE

Hebrews 13:17

"...FOR THEY WATCH FOR YOUR SOULS, AS THEY THAT MUST GIVE ACCOUNT..."

This book was not born from observation.

It was born from burden.

The words you are about to read did not come from a desire to critique the Church, but from a deep love for her. I write as one within the fold, not standing outside it. I write as a shepherd who understands the weight of responsibility, the complexity of leadership, and the holy calling to guard the people of God.

Because of that calling, some things cannot be softened.

Scripture says teachers and shepherds will give account. That truth shapes the tone of these pages. When the responsibility is heavy, the warning must be clear. This is not harshness — it is care. It is not accusation — it is accountability. It is not judgment — it is preparation.

Revival is not a light subject. It is holy

ground.

This message came to me as a sudden awareness of timing — a spiritual awakening to the reality that we are not waiting for revival as much as we are being called to readiness for it. What I sensed was not delay, but arrival. And with that arrival came a sobering realization: not every church will be positioned to receive what heaven is releasing.

That realization did not produce frustration.

It produced prayer.

This book is written from that place.

It is a call to leaders to examine the altar. A call to the Church to recover hunger. A call to repentance where pride has quietly settled. A call to surrender where control has grown comfortable. A call to remember that revival is not for our reputation, but for God's glory and the rescue of souls.

If you read these pages and feel conviction, receive it as invitation. If you feel exposed, let it lead to restoration. If you feel stirred, let it move you to prayer.

Because the purpose of this book is not to

declare who is missing revival.

It is to help ensure we do not.

May these words drive us lower before God, deeper in prayer, and closer to the fire of His presence.

It is revival time.

Let us be ready.

"Search me, O God, and know my heart: try me, and know my thoughts:
And see if there be any wicked way in me, and lead me in the way everlasting."
— Psalm 139:23–24

INTRODUCTION

Before My Feet Touched the Floor

Before my feet touched the floor that morning — before the day had formed its demands, before thought fully cleared — a sentence rose in my spirit with unusual clarity and weight:

It's revival time.

It did not feel emotional.
It did not feel dramatic.
It felt settled.

Like something already decided in heaven.

Not a prayer request.
Not a hopeful slogan.

Not religious excitement.

A declaration.

The kind that marks a moment.
The kind that signals a shift.
The kind that does not wait for earth's agreement because it has already been released from heaven.

But as that holy certainty settled, another truth followed — not loud, but sobering:

Many churches will miss it.

That tension is what birthed this book.

Because the tragedy of this hour will not be that God failed to move.
The tragedy will be that He moved — and some were not ready.

For generations, the Church has spoken about revival.

We have prayed for it.
Sung about it.
Preached about it.
Prophesied about it.

But what happens when revival is no longer a future hope — but a present moment?

What happens when heaven's calendar turns, and the season we longed for arrives...

yet our structures, hearts, and leadership cultures are not positioned to receive what we asked for?

This is the burden behind these pages.

This is not written as criticism of the Church.

It is written as a cry for the Church.

Not from anger — but from urgency.
Not to accuse — but to awaken.

Revival is not a series of powerful meetings.

It is divine interruption.

It is holy disruption.

It is the manifest nearness of God that confronts, convicts, purifies, restores, and sends.

And not every environment that welcomes excitement is prepared for encounter.

We can talk about revival and still resist it.
We can pray for fire and still protect what fire came to burn.

We can invite God to move and still confine Him to our comfort, traditions, structures, and preferences.

And heaven will not force its way where it

is only verbally welcomed but structurally resisted.

We are living in a prophetic hour.

There is a stirring beneath the surface. A hunger rising in places once indifferent. A shaking beginning in systems long untouched. The Spirit of God is moving with end-time urgency tied to harvest, repentance, and preparation.

But revival does not settle where it is discussed. It rests where it is yielded to.

Hosting revival is not about atmosphere — it is about alignment. It requires humility, repentance, surrendered leadership, burning altars, and a burden for souls.

Where these are absent, revival does not argue. It passes.

This book is a call to readiness. A call to examine not just what we say we want, but what we are actually prepared to receive. Because revival is not missed due to God's unwillingness. It is missed due to human unpreparedness.

Heaven is ready. The question is — are we?

"And that, knowing the time, that now it is

high time to awake out of sleep…"
— Romans 13:11

SECTION I — WHY REVIVAL IS MISSED

CHAPTER 1

When Comfort Becomes an Idol
How Ease Silences the Cry for More

Revival has never been comfortable.

It has never entered quietly, sat politely, and left everything the same. Revival does not exist to decorate what already is. It comes to disrupt, to expose, to awaken, and to realign. It shakes what has settled and confronts what has grown familiar.

And that is precisely why many churches will miss it.

Because comfort has become sacred.

In many places, the highest unspoken priority is not transformation — it is stability. Not holiness — but ease. Not conviction — but atmosphere. Churches have slowly and subtly shifted from being places of holy encounter to environments carefully curated to ensure people feel welcomed, relaxed, and undisturbed.

But revival does not come to soothe.
It comes to search.

Comfort tells people, "You are fine."
Revival declares, "Come higher."

Comfort avoids tension.
Revival creates holy tension.

Comfort protects routine.
Revival interrupts routine.

And where comfort sits on the throne, fire has nowhere to land.

The modern church has mastered the art of creating safe spiritual environments — but safety and surrender are not the same thing. People can sit in padded seats, enjoy well-crafted services, and leave emotionally uplifted while spiritually unchanged.

No one trembles.

No one weeps.
No one lingers.
No one wrestles with God.

The atmosphere is pleasant, but the altar is cold.

This is not because leaders do not love God. It is because, over time, systems begin to value what keeps things manageable. Services are structured to fit time slots. Messages are shaped to avoid discomfort. Moments of conviction are softened so no one feels exposed.

Yet revival has never asked, "Will this make people comfortable?"
It asks, "Will they yield?"

When comfort becomes the governing spirit of a house, repentance feels extreme. Intercession feels excessive. Extended prayer feels unnecessary. Tears feel emotional. Brokenness feels awkward.

But these are the very things revival is built upon.

Revival is born where people are willing to be undone.

It is carried by those who would rather

be convicted than entertained, corrected than applauded, purified than preserved. But where the culture of a church subtly communicates, "Do not go too deep," "Do not get too intense," "Do not disrupt the flow," revival senses resistance.

Not loud resistance.
Polite resistance.
Structured resistance.

And that kind is harder to confront.

The danger of comfort is not that it feels wrong. It feels right. It feels kind. It feels considerate. It feels wise. But when comfort replaces hunger, the church begins to desire peace more than power.

And heaven does not pour fire on what is trying to stay comfortable.

Fire burns.
Fire refines.
Fire exposes.

Fire does not coexist with the preservation of ease.

This is why revival often begins in unexpected places — prayer rooms, small gatherings, hidden spaces — where hunger outweighs preference. Where people cry out without a schedule. Where repentance is not edited. Where the presence of God is more important than the smoothness of the service.

Comfort keeps things predictable.
Revival makes things holy.

If the Church of this hour is to host the move of God, it must confront this idol. Not by becoming harsh, but by becoming hungry. Not by removing care, but by restoring consecration.

People must once again be willing to be searched.
Leaders must once again be willing to be corrected.
Services must once again make room for the unscripted.

Because revival does not visit where comfort is king.

It rests where the altar burns.

> "Woe to those who are at ease in Zion..."
> — AMOS 6:1

CHAPTER 2

When Image Replaces Glory
*Choosing Appearance Over the
Weight of His Presence*

Revival carries weight.

Not emotional weight.

Not atmospheric weight.

Glory weight.

The kind that cannot be manufactured, staged, or edited. The kind that silences rooms, exposes hearts, and leaves people aware that God Himself has drawn near.

But glory is heavy.

And image is light.

Image can be managed.
Glory cannot.

This is where many churches quietly lose alignment with revival. Not through rebellion. Not through denial of God. But through a subtle shift — from hosting His presence to managing perception.

We are living in an era where the Church has become visible in ways previous generations never imagined. Platforms, broadcasts, social media, branding, presentation — none of these are wrong in themselves. But when visibility becomes priority, glory becomes secondary.

Image asks, "How does this look?"
Glory asks, "Is God here?"

Image is concerned with impression.
Glory is concerned with encounter.

Image is crafted.
Glory descends.

And when a house becomes more attentive to how it is seen than to how God is received, revival senses restriction.

Because revival does not exist to make a

ministry look powerful.
It exists to make people holy.

In image-driven environments, leaders become careful. Not spiritually careful — publicly careful. Decisions are filtered through how they will be interpreted, shared, clipped, or discussed. Moments of conviction may be softened. Manifestations of brokenness may be hurried along. Silence may be uncomfortable. Tears may be redirected.

Not because there is no love for God — but because there is fear of losing control of how things appear.

But glory does not cooperate with image management.

Glory exposes.

It reveals what branding hides. It uncovers what polish conceals. It does not ask, "Will this affect attendance?" It asks, "Will this bring alignment?"

And where appearance is protected more than authenticity, the Spirit is subtly limited.

The tragedy is that image can look spiritual.

Excellence can mask emptiness.
Presentation can substitute for presence.
Momentum can imitate movement.

But heaven does not measure services by smoothness. It measures them by surrender.

Revival will not flow freely where everything must be contained within presentation standards. It will not be confined to camera angles, time limits, or aesthetic continuity. It does not arrive to enhance production — it comes to alter hearts.

And hearts do not change because things look impressive.
They change when glory makes them aware of God.

Throughout Scripture, when glory fell, image disappeared.

Priests could not stand to minister. Faces fell to the ground. Voices trembled. Plans stopped. The moment was no longer about who was leading, how things appeared, or what came next. It was about response.

But in image-centered cultures, response is controlled. Tears are managed. Conviction is shortened. The unscripted is minimized.

Because unscripted moments cannot be predicted.

And what cannot be predicted cannot be packaged.

Yet revival lives in the unscripted.

This does not mean excellence should disappear. It means excellence must bow. Presentation must serve presence, not replace it. Visibility must never outrank vulnerability before God.

When image leads, glory withdraws.

When glory leads, image becomes irrelevant.

Revival will not rest where reputation is guarded more fiercely than the altar. It will not settle where leaders fear looking weak more than they fear missing God.

Because glory is not concerned with looking strong.

It is concerned with making hearts right.

If this hour of revival is to be received, churches must shift their focus from how they are perceived to how they are positioned. From platform to prayer. From impression to intercession. From managing moments to yielding to movement.

Image can fill a room.
Only glory can change one.

And revival follows glory.

> "Ichabod... The glory is departed."
> — 1 Samuel 4:21

CHAPTER 3

The Pride That Silences Repentance
When Leaders Cannot Bow, Revival Cannot Flow

Revival never begins on the platform.
It begins at the altar of repentance.
Not public performance.
Not visible activity.
But hidden surrender.

Before revival ever touches a congregation, it touches leaders. Before fire falls on gatherings, it falls on hearts. And the doorway to that fire has always been the same:

Humility.

This is where many churches quietly miss their moment.

Not because they reject God.
Not because they deny truth.
But because pride has become too comfortable to confront.

Pride in the Church rarely looks loud or arrogant. It often looks polished, confident, and established. It hides behind experience, reputation, and spiritual history.

"We have been here a long time."
"We know how to do this."
"We have built something strong."

But revival does not come to affirm what we have built. It comes to examine it.

And pride resists examination.

Pride does not like being searched.
Pride does not like being corrected.
Pride does not like being told something must change.

Yet revival always begins with heaven saying, "Return."

The greatest danger of pride in leadership is not failure — it is the inability to admit drift. Systems can slowly shift. Focus can gradually move. Passion can cool in ways that are subtle and unintentional.

But when pride governs, leaders defend instead of discern. Correction feels like attack. Conviction feels like accusation. The call to repentance feels unnecessary.

"We are doing well."
"People are coming."
"Things are working."

But revival does not measure success by activity. It measures by alignment.

And alignment requires humility.

Throughout Scripture, whenever God prepared to move among His people, He first dealt with leaders. He confronted kings, priests, and prophets. He exposed hidden compromises. He called for repentance not just from the crowd, but from those entrusted with spiritual oversight.

Because leaders set the spiritual climate.

If leaders will not bow, the house will not bend.

If leaders will not repent, the people will not tremble.

If leaders will not be broken, the altar will

not burn.

Revival cannot flow through vessels that must always appear strong.

Pride insists on maintaining image. Humility is willing to lose face before men in order to find favour with God.

Pride protects position.
Humility protects presence.

Pride says, "We are fine."
Humility says, "Search us."

The Spirit does not bypass leadership out of disrespect. He confronts it out of love. But where that confrontation is resisted, revival pauses. Not because God withdraws, but because access is restricted.

Heaven will not force its way into a house that refuses to bow.

One of the clearest signs that pride has silenced repentance is the absence of tears in leadership. When was the last time leaders publicly wept, not for effect, but from genuine brokenness? When was the last time a shepherd stood before the people and said, "We need God. We have drifted. Let us return"?

Revival does not diminish leaders. It purifies them. It does not strip authority. It sanctifies it.

But pride fears exposure more than it desires purification.

And where pride stands, repentance stays silent.

If the Church is to receive this hour of revival, leaders must lead the way — not in confidence, but in consecration. Not in strength, but in surrender. They must model brokenness, hunger, and willingness to be corrected.

Because the fire that purifies the people first passes through the hands of those who carry the altar.

And revival always follows humility.

"God resisteth the proud, but giveth grace unto the humble."
— James 4:6

CHAPTER 4

Control vs the Move of the Spirit
When Order Is Used to Restrain the Holy Spirit

One of the quietest killers of revival is not sin in the pew — it is control in the pulpit.

Revival is not resisted only by unbelief. It is often restricted by leadership that loves God, but does not trust Him enough to release the reins.

And this is where we must speak plainly.

Some leaders pray for revival while simultaneously building systems that would never allow it.

They want the Spirit — scheduled.
They want power — predictable.
They want God to move — but within the boundaries of comfort, timing, and personal oversight.

But revival has never followed a program.

Control in leadership rarely announces itself. It hides behind words like "order," "structure," and "excellence." And while God is a God of order, human control and divine order are not the same thing.

Divine order makes room for the Spirit.

Human control makes room only for what leadership can manage.

And many churches have become so tightly managed that nothing unscripted survives.

Prayer must end on time.

Worship must follow the run sheet.

Moments of conviction must be shortened.

Expressions of brokenness must not disrupt flow.

Everything must move smoothly.

But revival is not smooth.

When the Spirit begins to move deeply, things stretch. People linger. Tears come. Silence falls. Schedules shift. The atmosphere grows heavy. And leaders must decide in those moments whether they will guard the program — or guard the presence.

Too often, the program wins.

Because leaders fear losing control of what happens next. They fear disorder, emotionalism, or things they cannot explain. They fear how it may look. They fear stepping into territory where they are no longer the primary drivers of the moment.

But revival always moves beyond what leaders can orchestrate.

If every expression of the Spirit must pass through leadership comfort levels, revival will suffocate.

Let us speak directly.

Some leaders trust their outlines more than they trust the Spirit. They trust their ability to guide the service more than God's ability to guide His people. They feel responsible for maintaining momentum, protecting the atmosphere, and keeping everything "in hand."

But revival does not sit in human hands.

And leaders who cannot release control often do not realize they are the bottleneck. They pray, "Lord, move," while quietly holding the door shut.

Control says, "I must understand it."

The Spirit says, "Follow Me."

Control says, "Keep it contained."
The Spirit says, "Let it flow."

Another danger of control is selective permission. Leaders may welcome the Spirit when He moves in familiar ways, through familiar people, in familiar expressions. But when He moves through unexpected vessels — a young believer, a quiet intercessor, someone outside the inner circle — resistance appears.

Why?

Because control prefers known channels.

But revival does not ask who has seniority. It asks who is surrendered.

Leaders who cannot rejoice when God uses someone outside their structure reveal insecurity more than stewardship. And insecurity dressed as authority is still control.

This is not a call for chaos. It is a call for surrender.

True spiritual leadership does not disappear in revival — it shifts posture. It becomes more sensitive, more prayerful, more yielded. It learns to recognize when God is doing something deeper than the plan.

But leaders who must always steer will struggle to host what they cannot direct.

Revival is not impressed with leadership strength. It responds to leadership surrender.

If the Church is to receive this hour, leaders must ask

hard questions:

Do we truly want God to move — even if it disrupts us?

Even if it extends beyond our schedule?

Even if it challenges our control?

Even if we are no longer the center of the moment?

Because revival will not be contained in carefully constructed boundaries.

It flows where space is given.

And space is created when leaders step back, bow low, and let the Spirit lead.

"Where the Spirit of the Lord is, there is liberty."
— 2 Corinthians 3:17

CHAPTER 5

Entertainment and the Golden Calf Church
When Performance Replaces the Presence of God

There is a form of worship that looks alive… but is hollow.

It is loud but not weighty.

Expressive but not transformative.

Impressive but not purifying.

And it is one of the greatest reasons many churches will miss revival.

Because what we call worship has, in many

places, become performance.

When Moses went up the mountain, the people grew restless. They wanted something visible, something engaging, something they could gather around and celebrate. So, they built a golden calf. They called it worship. They sang. They rejoiced. They gathered in excitement.

But God was not in it.

It was energetic.
It was collective.
It was emotionally charged.

But it was man-made.

The golden calf was not an act of rebellion against worship — it was a replacement for the presence of God.

And the Church must be careful not to repeat this pattern.

Today, gatherings can be vibrant, creative, and highly engaging. Lights move. Music swells. Atmospheres are built. Crowds respond. And yet, beneath the activity, there can be a quiet absence of holy weight.

People feel something.
But they are not changed.

They leave stirred, but not surrendered.
Excited, but not examined.
Uplifted, but not undone.

Entertainment touches emotions.
Revival confronts the soul.

And the difference between the two is the presence of God.

Entertainment is easier to produce than encounter.

It can be rehearsed, designed, perfected. It depends on talent, creativity, and presentation. And none of those things are wrong — until they begin to replace the pursuit of God's manifest presence.

When excellence becomes the goal instead of an offering, worship shifts from surrender to performance.

And leaders must ask the hard question:

Are we hosting God — or hosting an experience?

Revival does not thrive in performance culture.

Because performance is about being seen.
Revival is about seeing Him.

Performance asks, "Did they enjoy it?"
Revival asks, "Did they encounter God?"

Performance keeps focus on the stage.
Revival pulls attention to the altar.

In performance-driven environments, silence is uncomfortable. Waiting feels awkward. Brokenness disrupts flow. Tears slow momentum. Repentance feels heavy.

So, everything moves quickly.

But revival moves deeply.

The golden calf was not built because people hated God. It was built because they wanted something immediate, visible, and controllable. Something that responded to them, rather than requiring surrender from them.

The danger today is similar.

When gatherings revolve around how people feel rather than how God is received, worship becomes centered on experience rather than encounter.

And revival cannot live where people are being entertained instead of being transformed.

Let us be clear.

Music is not the problem. Creativity is not the problem. Expression is not the problem. The problem is when the goal shifts from honoring God to engaging people.

Because revival is not sustained by excitement.

It is sustained by consecration.

When the Church prefers the energy of the crowd over the weight of His presence, it has built something that looks like worship — but lacks the fire of heaven.

And fire does not fall on golden calves.

If this end-time revival is to be received, the Church must return to worship that costs something. Worship that trembles. Worship that lingers. Worship that makes space for conviction, repentance, and holy awe.

Because revival does not ride on performance.

It rests on altars.

"These people draw near to Me with their mouth, and honor Me with their lips; but their heart is far from Me."
— Matthew 15:8

CHAPTER 6

A Church Without a Burden for Souls
When the Harvest Is Forgotten, the Fire Fades

Revival is not sent for church growth. It is sent for soul harvest.

And this is where many churches reveal, without realizing it, that they are not ready for the move they claim to desire.

Because revival is not measured by how full the building is — but by how broken the heart is for the lost.

It is possible for a church to be active, organized, and spiritually expressive, yet carry little burden for those outside its walls.

Programs may run. Events may happen. Services may be well attended. But if the cry for souls is absent, the church has lost alignment with heaven's priority.

Revival does not come to entertain the found.

It comes to rescue the lost.

When the Church becomes primarily inward-focused — concerned with preferences, comfort, and internal culture — it may still function, but it no longer reflects the heart of God in revival.

Because revival carries urgency for those who are perishing.

The Spirit of God does not move deeply where the Church is satisfied with itself.

He moves where there is groaning.

Groaning in prayer.
Groaning in intercession.
Groaning for sons and daughters, neighbors and nations.

When was the last time leaders wept over souls more than over numbers? When was the last time prayer gatherings sounded like labour rooms rather than planning sessions?

Revival is born in travail.

And travail is rare in comfort-driven Christianity.

A church without a burden for souls begins to treat revival as an internal blessing rather than an outward assignment. It becomes about atmosphere, experience, and spiritual enjoyment rather than mission.

But revival is not a retreat.

It is a deployment.

It sends people out. It pushes believers beyond their circles. It ignites evangelism. It awakens compassion. It makes the lost impossible to ignore.

Where that fire is missing, revival becomes reduced to meetings — and meetings alone cannot carry heaven's agenda.

Let us speak plainly.

Some churches pray for revival, but do not create space for evangelism. They sing about harvest but do not sow. They celebrate community while forgetting commission.

But revival and evangelism are inseparable.

When God moves in power, hearts break

for people. Conversations change. Priorities shift. Time is made. Prayer becomes specific. Names are lifted. Streets matter.

A church that does not ache for the lost may enjoy spiritual activity — but it is not positioned for revival.

Heaven's heart beats for the perishing.

And revival aligns the Church with that heartbeat.

When souls matter again, programs adjust. When eternity becomes real again, schedules shift. When compassion returns, complacency dies.

Revival will not settle where there is no burden.

Because the fire of God burns hottest where love for the lost burns strongest.

If the Church in this hour is to receive revival, it must recover holy desperation for souls. Not as a ministry department — but as a defining passion. Not as an event — but as identity.

Because revival does not belong to the comfortable.

It belongs to those who feel the weight of

eternity.

"He that goeth forth and weepeth, bearing precious seed, shall doubtless come again with rejoicing, bringing his sheaves with him."

— Psalm 126:6

CHAPTER 7

Tradition
The Respectable Resistance

Not all resistance to revival looks rebellious.

Some of it looks respectable.

It is dressed in history, structure, and familiarity. It speaks the language of faithfulness. It carries the comfort of what has "always been done." And because it feels safe, it is rarely examined.

This is the power of tradition.

Tradition is not evil in itself. It can preserve truth, carry heritage, and provide stability. But when tradition becomes the authority instead of the Spirit, it quietly becomes resistance.

Not loud resistance.
Not aggressive resistance.
Respectable resistance.

And revival often stalls in its presence.

One of the most dangerous phrases in the Church is not heresy — it is familiarity.

"We've never done it that way."
"That's not how we do things here."
"We don't move like that."

These statements do not sound hostile. They sound reasonable. But revival does not move according to what has always been. It moves according to what heaven is doing now.

Tradition protects the past.
Revival prepares the future.

And when the Church clings to what was more tightly than it listens for what God is saying, it slowly becomes anchored to memory instead of movement.

The problem with tradition is not that it remembers. It is that it can resist renewal. What once began as a move of God can harden into a method. What was once a fresh expression can become a fixed expectation.

Then anything outside that expectation feels strange, excessive, or unnecessary.

But revival rarely looks like the last one.

God does not repeat Himself to make people comfortable. He moves in ways that stretch, challenge, and sometimes unsettle. And where tradition governs more than the Spirit, stretching feels like error instead of growth.

Tradition often disguises itself as wisdom.

"We don't want extremes."
"We must stay balanced."
"We've seen things get out of hand."

And while discernment is necessary, fear of the unfamiliar can become the real motivator. Instead of asking, "Is God in this?" the question becomes, "Does this fit our pattern?"

Revival will not shrink itself to fit inherited expectations.

It calls the Church to adjust, not God.

Respectable resistance is difficult to confront because it feels right. It honors heritage. It values order. It seeks to avoid mistakes. But if tradition becomes the gatekeeper, the Spirit becomes a guest instead of Lord.

And revival does not ask to be accommodated.

It asks to lead.

When tradition rules, revival is evaluated. When the Spirit rules, tradition is re-examined.

And not everything that is old is sacred.

This is not a call to abandon truth. It is a call to remain sensitive. To recognize that God's methods may shift while His message remains. To understand that what carried one season may not carry the next.

The Church must learn to hold methods loosely and obedience tightly.

Because revival often arrives wrapped in unfamiliar expression, new voices, and unexpected rhythms. And those who insist on yesterday's form may miss today's fire.

If the Church is to receive this hour of revival, it must honor its history without being imprisoned by it. It must be willing to ask not just, "What have we done?" but

"What is God doing now?"

Because respectable resistance is still resistance. And revival will not force its way through doors that tradition keeps closed.

"Thus, saith the Lord, Stand ye in the ways, and see, and ask for the old paths... but they said, We will not walk therein."
— Jeremiah 6:16

CHAPTER 8

Why Revival Moves Elsewhere
When Readiness Determines Resting Places

Revival is not random.

It is not accidental.

It is not sentimental.

It is not drawn to noise, numbers, or notoriety.

Revival is responsive.

It responds to hunger.
It responds to humility.
It responds to repentance.
It responds to surrender.

And when these are absent, revival does not

fight to stay. It moves.

Throughout history, whenever God has poured out His Spirit, the move has rarely remained where it began. It has shifted, travelled, and settled in places least expected. Not because God is unstable, but because people are.

When hearts grow cold, altars grow quiet. When leaders grow comfortable, prayer grows shallow. When churches grow satisfied, hunger fades.

And revival, which feeds on hunger, looks for another place to land.

Revival does not belong to reputation.

It belongs to readiness.

A church may have history, influence, resources, and recognition. But if the fire on the altar is gone, revival will not be persuaded to remain because of what once was.

Heaven does not honor legacy over alignment.

The question revival asks is not, "What did you do before?"
It asks, "Are you hungry now?"

There are moments when God moves through a place powerfully, but the people begin to protect the memory of the move instead of pursuing the God of the move. They build identity around what happened rather than pressing into what is happening.

The result is preservation instead of pursuit.

But revival is not sustained by memory.

It is sustained by ongoing surrender.

Where surrender slows, revival lifts.

Let us speak plainly.

Some churches will talk about revival while quietly resisting every condition required for it. They will celebrate stories of past moves while avoiding present repentance. They will admire hunger in others while protecting comfort in themselves.

And revival will pass them by — not in anger, but in response to openness elsewhere.

Because somewhere, someone is praying.

Somewhere, someone is weeping.

Somewhere, someone is hungry enough to be undone.

And revival always moves toward hunger.

This is the sobering truth.

God is not withholding revival.

He is searching for vessels.

If leaders will bow, if altars will burn, if prayer will deepen, if souls will matter again — revival will settle. But if pride stands, comfort reigns, control governs, image leads, performance replaces presence, and tradition resists — revival will move on.

Not because God is absent.

But because space was not made.

Revival is not missed because heaven failed.

It is missed because earth was unprepared.

And the greatest tragedy of this hour would not be the absence of revival — but the presence of revival that we were not positioned to receive.

But the story is not finished.

Because revival is still moving.

And doors can still open.

"The eyes of the Lord run to and fro throughout the whole earth, to show Himself strong on behalf of those whose

heart is loyal to Him."
— 2 Chronicles 16:9

SECTION II — UNDERSTANDING REVIVAL

CHAPTER 9

The Nature of Revival Fire
What Revival Is and What It Is Not

Before the Church can receive revival, it must understand revival.

Because many are expecting something God never promised, while resisting the very thing He intends to send.

Revival has been reduced in some minds to excitement, momentum, or visible activity. But revival is not measured by volume, crowd size, or emotional intensity. Those things may accompany it — but they do not define it.

Revival is not noise.

It is fire. And fire does not entertain. It consumes.

What Revival Is Not!

Revival is not a series of powerful meetings.

Meetings can be scheduled. Revival cannot. Meetings can inspire. Revival transforms. Meetings may stir emotions for a moment. Revival rearranges priorities for a lifetime.

Revival is not hype!

Hype rises quickly and fades just as fast. Revival goes deep. It lingers. It changes the spiritual temperature of a people, not just the atmosphere of a room.

Revival is not personality-driven!

It does not depend on charisma, gifting, or influence. It may flow through vessels, but it is not sustained by them. When revival is tied to a personality, it becomes fragile. When it is anchored in God's presence, it becomes enduring.

Revival is not entertainment!

It does not exist to engage people's senses or produce emotional experiences.

Entertainment makes people feel good. Revival makes people aware of God — and awareness of God produces repentance.

Revival is not numbers!

Crowds can gather for many reasons. But revival is seen in brokenness, confession, restitution, hunger for holiness, and burden for souls.

If people leave excited but unchanged, stirred but not surrendered, inspired but not convicted — revival has not yet come.

What Revival Is!

Revival is the manifest presence of God returning a people to Himself.

It is God drawing near in such a way that sin cannot hide, pride cannot stand, and indifference cannot survive.

Revival brings conviction.

Not condemnation, but deep awareness. People become sensitive to what once felt normal. Casual compromise becomes uncomfortable. Prayer becomes necessary. Worship becomes weighty.

Revival brings repentance.

Not surface apologies, but genuine turning.

Habits break. Relationships are restored. Hidden sins are confessed. Priorities shift. Holiness becomes desirable, not restrictive.

Revival brings restoration.

Things long dormant awaken. Faith rises. Love deepens. The Word comes alive. Prayer becomes fire, not formality.

Revival brings hunger.

A hunger that meetings cannot satisfy. A hunger for God Himself. A hunger that pulls people into prayer rooms, not just gatherings. A hunger that lingers after services end.

Revival brings mission.

The lost become visible again. Evangelism becomes natural. Compassion increases. The Church moves outward, not just inward.

Revival fire is holy.

It does not only warm — it purifies. It burns what flesh built. It exposes what religion covered. It consumes what pride protected.

And this is why some resist it. Because fire does not negotiate.

It does not ask what may remain. It burns what must go so that what is of God can stand.

Many want revival's excitement without revival's exposure. They want the joy but not the cleansing. They want the movement but not the surrender.

But revival cannot be separated from fire.

And fire always changes what it touches.

Revival does not need to be advertised, because fire is self-advertising.

If the Church is to receive the revival fire this hour, it must lay down its false expectations. It must stop looking for revival to look impressive and start allowing revival to make it holy.

Because revival is not sent to make the Church louder.

It is sent to make the Church like Christ.

And that requires fire.

"For our God is a consuming fire."
— Hebrews 12:29

CHAPTER 10

The Cost of Revival
"What Fire Requires Before It Falls"

Many churches say they want revival. Few understand the cost.

Revival is not only a visitation — it is a surrender. It does not come simply because people desire it. It rests where people yield to it. And yielding always costs something.

Revival is free in one sense — it is God's grace. But hosting revival requires sacrifice.

And sacrifice is where many quietly step

back.

Revival costs time.

It does not fit neatly into tight schedules or rigid service structures. When God begins to move, meetings stretch. Prayer deepens. Waiting becomes necessary. Leaders must choose between efficiency and encounter.

Some churches protect their timetables more than they pursue His presence.

But revival cannot be rushed.

It lingers where people linger.

Revival costs reputation.

When God moves deeply, things may look unusual. Tears flow. Silence falls. Conviction settles. Leaders must be willing to appear weak, emotional, or out of control in the eyes of observers.

But leaders who protect their image more than they protect the presence will quietly shut revival down.

Because revival is not concerned with how things appear.

It is concerned with how hearts are aligned.

Revival costs control.

Plans must bend. Agendas must yield. Leaders must recognize when God is doing something beyond their outline and step aside rather than step in.

But stepping aside requires trust — trust that God knows how to lead His people without constant human management.

And that trust costs pride.

Revival costs comfort.

It exposes sin. It confronts compromise. It calls for holiness. It unsettles what has become normal. It challenges spiritual laziness. It demands consecration.

Many want the joy of revival without the purification of revival.

But fire warms and burns.

It is not selective.

Revival costs leadership ego.

In seasons of revival, attention shifts from personalities to presence. Leaders must rejoice when God uses others. They must be willing to decrease so that Christ is seen.

But ego resists disappearing.

And revival cannot rest where leadership

must remain the focus.

Revival costs ongoing surrender.

It is not sustained by one altar call, one meeting, or one emotional moment. It requires daily yielding, daily humility, daily prayer, daily obedience.

When churches celebrate the start of revival but resist the lifestyle that sustains it, the fire fades.

Because revival is not an event.

It is a condition of the heart.

This is why many pray for revival but do not host it. They desire the move, but not the dying. They want the blessing, but not the breaking. They seek the fire, but resist the altar.

But revival does not rest where sacrifice is optional.

It rests where surrender is normal.

If the Church in this hour is to receive the end-time outpouring, it must count the cost honestly. Not emotionally, but intentionally. It must choose presence over preference, obedience over optics, surrender over security.

Because revival is a gift.

But hosting it is a decision.

"If any man will come after Me, let him deny himself, and take up his cross daily, and follow Me."
— Luke 9:23

CHAPTER 11

Preparing the Altar Again
Returning to the Place Where Fire Falls

Revival does not begin with excitement.

It begins with repair.

Before fire fell in Scripture, altars were restored. Before God answered by fire, something broken had to be rebuilt. Because revival is not sustained by enthusiasm — it rests on consecration.

And consecration always begins at the altar.

The altar represents surrender.

It is where pride is laid down, where sin is confessed, where flesh is denied, where God is sought above all else. When altars are neglected, revival becomes impossible. Not because God is unwilling — but because space has not been made.

Many churches have platforms.
Few have altars.

There is movement, sound, and structure — but where is the place where hearts are truly yielded? Where is the culture of repentance? Where is the expectation that God will search us, correct us, and change us?

Revival returns when altars return.

Preparing the altar again means restoring prayer.

Not rushed prayer.
Not ceremonial prayer.
But desperate, dependent, waiting prayer.

Prayer that lingers. Prayer that groans. Prayer that does not move on until heaven responds. Revival is born in prayer closets long before it is seen in public gatherings.

When prayer becomes optional, revival becomes distant.

Preparing the altar again means restoring repentance.

Not as a rare response to failure, but as a normal posture of the heart. A church prepared for revival is a church quick to humble itself, quick to forgive, quick to confess.

Where repentance is absent, pride remains. And pride is dry ground.

Fire falls on humility.

Preparing the altar again means restoring leadership surrender.

Leaders must be the first to kneel. The first to be corrected. The first to model hunger. The first to step aside when God moves beyond plans.

If leaders rebuild the altar in their own lives, the house will follow.

But if leaders remain busy managing while neglecting their own consecration, the altar stays broken.

Preparing the altar again means making space.

Space in services for the unscripted. Space in schedules for prayer. Space in hearts for conviction. Space in leadership for the Spirit to interrupt.

Revival does not squeeze into crowded agendas.

It fills surrendered space.

This is not about returning to old methods.

It is about returning to first love.

When love for God becomes central again — not ministry success, not numbers, not reputation — the altar is rebuilt. And when the altar is rebuilt, fire follows.

Because God responds to preparation.

He responds to humility.

He responds to surrender.

The Church does not need to manufacture revival.

It needs to repair the altar.

And when the altar is ready, heaven knows.

"And Elijah said… Come near unto me. And he repaired the altar of the Lord that was broken down."
— 1 Kings 18:30

SECTION III — THE INVITATION

CHAPTER 12

It Is Not Too Late
The Door of Mercy Is Still Open

After warning comes invitation.
After exposure comes opportunity.
After conviction comes grace.

This message has been weighty because the hour is weighty. But the purpose of warning is not condemnation — it is preparation. God does not reveal what hinders revival to shame His Church. He reveals it to clear the way.

And the way is still open.

Revival is not gone.

It is not withheld.

It is not reserved for another generation.

It is moving now.

But God is not looking for perfect churches. He is looking for willing ones. Not churches that have never drifted, but churches that will return. Not leaders who have never failed, but leaders who will bow.

The door is not closed.

It is waiting to be opened.

The greatest danger is not having missed yesterday's opportunity. The greatest danger is believing it is too late today.

But God's mercy meets humility.

When a church turns, heaven responds. When leaders humble themselves, grace flows. When altars are rebuilt, fire falls. When prayer deepens, presence returns. When souls matter again, power moves.

Revival is not earned.

But readiness matters.

This is the mercy of God.

He does not announce revival to mock

the Church's weakness. He announces it to awaken the Church's responsibility. He calls His people not to observe the hour, but to step into it.

Every barrier named in this book can be removed.

Comfort can give way to hunger.
Image can bow to glory.
Pride can yield to repentance.
Control can surrender to the Spirit.
Entertainment can return to encounter.
Tradition can submit to obedience.
Altars can be rebuilt.

Nothing stands if hearts bow.

The end-time move of God will not be limited to one location, one stream, or one expression. It will flow where people are willing — in large places and small ones, in cities and hidden rooms, among leaders and unknown believers.

The question is not, "Will revival come?"

The question is, "Will we respond?"

Because heaven is ready.

The fire is ready.

The Spirit is moving.

And the invitation still stands.

Let this be the prayer of this hour:

Search us.
Humble us.
Cleanse us.
Burn again.

Because it is revival time.

And it is not too late.

"If My people, which are called by My name, shall humble themselves, and pray, and seek My face, and turn from their wicked ways; then will I hear from heaven, and will forgive their sin, and will heal their land."
— 2 Chronicles 7:14

EPILOGUE

A Prayer for the Altar

Lord,

If there is anything in us that resists Your move, show us.

If pride stands, reveal it.
If comfort dulls us, awaken us to it.
If tradition blinds us, open our eyes.
If control restrains us, teach us how to trust You.

Search the hidden places and give us courage to respond.

Touch what we have avoided and lead us into surrender.

Burn what You did not build, and show us how to lay it down.

Repair the altar in us again — and teach us how to keep it burning.

Let prayer become fire, not form.
Let worship carry weight, not noise.
Let repentance be normal, not rare.
Let holiness be desired, not resisted.
Give us hearts that tremble at Your Word.
Give us leaders who bow low.
Give us churches that hunger more for Your presence than for their own preservation.

Do not let us admire revival from a distance.

Show us how to be ready when You pass by.

Show us how to make room.
Show us how to yield.
Show us how to follow.

Because it is revival time. And we want to be ready. Amen.

ABOUT THE AUTHOR

Dr. Letitia McPherson is a seasoned minister of the Gospel, teacher of the Word, and spiritual leader with decades of experience shepherding God's people. Known for her clear biblical teaching, prophetic insight, and deep pastoral care, she carries a burden for spiritual awakening, leadership integrity, and the restoration of the altar in the Church.

Her ministry is marked by a passion for revival, prayer, and the uncompromised truth of Scripture. She speaks with both conviction and compassion, calling believers and leaders alike to deeper surrender, greater humility, and renewed hunger for the presence of God.

Dr. McPherson's work consistently bridges the prophetic and the practical — confronting spiritual complacency while guiding the Church toward readiness for what God is doing in this hour. She writes not as a critic, but as a shepherd, carrying the weight of accountability before God and love for His people.

She continues to teach, mentor, and serve with a heart fixed on seeing lives transformed, leaders strengthened, and the Body of Christ aligned with heaven's purposes.

To learn more, connect, or explore additional resources, visit:

www.godsgracebookstore.com

If this book - It's Revival Times touched your
heart, I would love to hear from you.

Your reflections and reviews help this message of
God's grace reach others who need it too.

Please consider leaving a review on Amazon or wherever you
purchased this book. Just a few heartfelt words go a long way.

You can also follow or write to me at:
legacyofgracemovement2025025@yahoo.com
https://www.facebook.com/godsgraceistand
https://www.facebook.com/godsgraceistand
https://www.bygodsgraceistand.com
From my heart to yours—thank you for reading.

"May God's grace keep your heart awakened, your altar burning,
and your life aligned with His move in this revival hour."

With much love and Appreciation,

Dr. Letitia McPherso

More Books by this Author

IT'S REVIVAL TIME

All available on Amazon or @www.godsgracebookstore.com

> "There are three persons living in each of us: the one we think we are, the one other people think we are, and the one God knows we are."
>
> — Leonard Ravenhill, <u>Why Revival Tarries</u> —

Made in the USA
Coppell, TX
28 February 2026

72541574R00056